The book is in three parts.

Your child's teacher will tell you when to start a new part.

Each part can be used for a whole term.
The activities can be done in any order.
Some activities can be done several times.

Please help your child fill in the date when they finish an activity.

I did this activity on ___Tuesday 19th Nov.___

There are more activities for Blue Level in the Copymasters and Games Pack.
Your child's teacher may send some of these home, too.

PART 1

There are eight activities in Part I.

They will help you to practise:
- counting to 50, forwards and backwards, in Is and in 5s.
- spelling numbers one to ten.
- using money.
- adding and taking away with numbers up to 20.

Do each activity as often as you want to.

NAME:

HOME MATHS

ROSE GRIFFITHS

Using this book

This book is aimed at helping your child to build on the maths they learn at school. We hope you and your child enjoy the activities in this book.

You will need:

a dice

a calculator

Ten pences, pennies and other coins

playing cards

card, paper, pencils and scissors

counters, buttons or pasta wheels

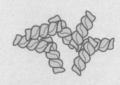

pasta shapes or dried beans for counting

Collect six plastic bottles to use as skittles.

Roll up a pair of socks to use as a ball.

How many can you knock down with one throw?

How many are left standing?

If you collect 4 more bottles, you can try again with 10 skittles!

I did this activity on

-------------------------------   -------------------------------

Number links

These numbers are linked.

2 4 6

2 + 4 = 6	4 + 2 = 6
6 − 2 = 4	6 − 4 = 2

Use pennies or fingers to help you:

2 + 3 = ___   3 + 5 = ___

3 + 2 = ___   5 + 3 = ___

5 − 2 = ___   8 − 5 = ___

5 − 3 = ___   8 − 3 = ___

3 + 4 = ___

4 + 3 = ___

7 − 4 = ___

7 − 3 = ___

3 + 6 = ___

6 + 3 = ___

9 − 3 = ___

9 − 6 = ___

Make up four sums with these:

	+		=	
	+		=	
	−		=	
	−		=	

Make up four sums with these:

	+		=	
	+		=	
	−		=	
	−		=	

I finished these pages on _____

Practise counting with a partner.
You need 50 things to count.

I'm using dried beans.

- Say a number between 10 and 50.
  Your partner has to give you that
  many things as quickly as possible.

27

- Check them.
  Then let your partner choose a
  number for you!

I did this activity on

------------------------------   ------------------------------

------------------------------   ------------------------------

Spelling numbers

1 one	
2 two	
3 three	
4 four	
5 five	
6 six	
7 seven	
8 eight	
9 nine	
10 ten	

Ask four people you know:

Which number from 1 to 10 is the <u>hardest</u> to spell?

Draw each person.
Which number did they say?
Make sure <u>you</u> spell it correctly!

I finished this page on _____

What's 1 + 2?

It's 3!
I don't have to
work that out.
I just <u>know</u> it,
off by heart.

If you do a sum lots of times,
you can learn the answer off by heart.

1 2 + 1 = ____

2 0 + 3 = ____

3 1 + 4 = ____

4 5 + 0 = ____

5 5 + 0 = ____

6 5 + 0 = ____

7 5 + 0 = ____

8 5 + 0 = ____

9 3 + 1 = ____

Check

Which ones
do you know
off by heart?

Try the same sums twice to help you learn them.

1	3 + 3 = ____	8	4 + 3 = ____
2	2 + 2 = ____	9	2 + 4 = ____
3	5 + 2 = ____	10	2 + 2 = ____
4	4 + 3 = ____	11	5 + 2 = ____
5	1 + 3 = ____	12	3 + 3 = ____
6	2 + 4 = ____	13	3 + 2 = ____
7	3 + 2 = ____	14	1 + 3 = ____

Now ask someone to read these out loud for you!

1	1 + 3	3	0 + 4	5	2 + 2
2	3 + 3	4	3 + 2	6	5 + 2

I finished these pages on _____

Set up a shoe shop.

1 Make three or four £10 notes.

2 Find about 15 counters or buttons.

You can pretend these are £1 coins.

3 Find some shoes...

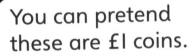

4 Make price labels for the shoes. Nothing more than £19!

5 Find someone to come shopping.

How much change?

You can count up...

or take away

£7 + £3 = £10

| 1 | 0 | − | 7 | = | 3 |

so there is £3 change

I did this activity on

---------------------------------   -----------------------------------

---------------------------------   -----------------------------------

Fives

Fill in the missing numbers.

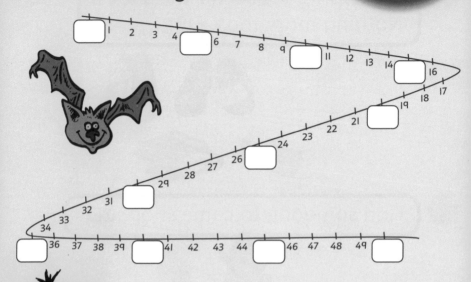

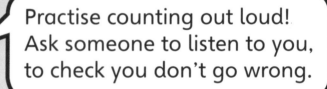

Practise counting out loud!
Ask someone to listen to you,
to check you don't go wrong.

- Count from 50 to 0. 50, 49, 48, ...

- Count in 5s from 0 to 50. 0, 5, 10, 15, ...

- Count in 5s from 50 to 0. 50, 45, 40, ...

Find 50 things to count.

I'm using pasta twists!

Use 20 pasta twists. Put them in rows of 5.
Count them one at a time. Then count them in 5s.

1, 2, 3, 4, 5		5
6, 7, 8, 9, 10		10
11, 12, 13, 14, 15		15
16, 17, 18, 19, 20		20

Add more rows of 5 until you have 50!

I did these activities on

------------------------------   ------------------------------

You need all the cards numbered 3 to 10 from a pack of cards.

You can play on your own or with a partner.

Before you start, shuffle the cards.

Put the pile of cards face down on the table.

Take two cards.
Add these numbers.

You can use fingers
or pennies to help you.

5 add 7
makes 12.

Check with a calculator.

    12 ✓

- Keep the cards if you are right.
- If not, put them back
  at the bottom of the pack.

I played this game on

------------------------------   ------------------------------

PART 2

There are nine activities in Part 2.

They will help you practise:

- counting to 60, forwards and backwards, in Is, 5s, and I0s.
- spelling numbers eleven to twenty.
- adding and taking away with numbers up to 24...or more!
- using money.
- telling the time (hours and half hours).

Do each activity as often as you want to.

And you can still do any from Part I!

Spelling to twenty

11 eleven
12 twelve
13 thirteen
14 fourteen
15 fifteen

16 sixteen
17 seventeen
18 eighteen
19 nineteen
20 twenty

Write the number and the word.

12 twelve

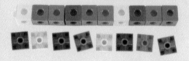

Ask someone to test you on all the spellings!

I finished this page on

I save pennies.

I put them in piles of ten to count.

There is 25p here.

You need 50p in pennies in a bowl.

Take a big handful from the bowl.

How much money have you got?

Put the pennies in piles of ten, to help you count them.

Do this a few times.
Use <u>two</u> hands if you want to!

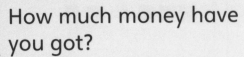

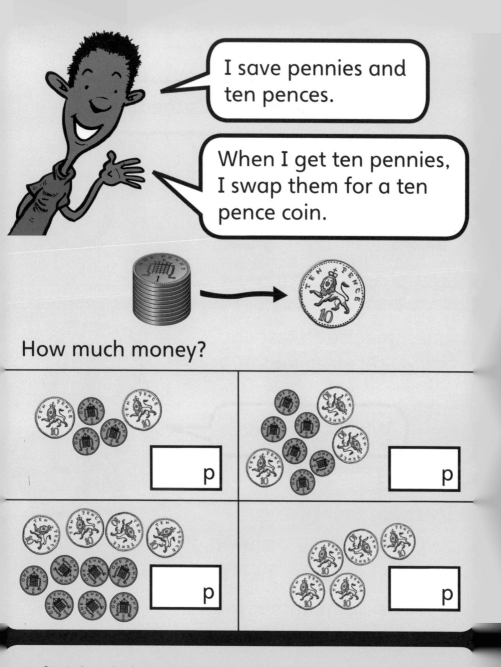

I save pennies and ten pences.

When I get ten pennies, I swap them for a ten pence coin.

How much money?

p

p

p

p

I finished these pages on _____

What's the time?

_____ o'clock   Half past _____   _____

Ask someone to test you.
Use a real clock with hands.

What's the time?

Try these times:

seven o'clock   eleven o'clock

half past seven   half past eleven

Make up some more, too!

I finished this page on _____

Fingers

Fingers can help you take away.

7 – 3 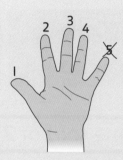  = 4

Do these with your fingers:

8 – 2 = ____   10 – 5 = ____

5 – 3 = ____   7 – 4 = ____

9 – 4 = ____   6 – 2 = ____

5 – 2 = ____   9 – 5 = ____

Now try them again, <u>without</u> your fingers.

10 – 5 = ____   8 – 2 = ____

7 – 4 = ____   5 – 3 = ____

6 – 2 = ____   9 – 4 = ____

9 – 5 = ____   5 – 2 = ____

I finished this page on _____

Take the money

Collect £5

Collect £20

Collect £5

Collect £10

Collect £15

Collect £10

Collect £5

Collect £10

A game for 1 or 2 people.

£5 BANK OF ENGLAND
London FIVE
BANK OF ENGLAND

How much money did you get?

I played this game on

------------------------------   ------------------------------

Collect
£15

Collect
£5

START HERE

Make six £10 notes and six £5 notes.
You need a dice and a counter each.

FINISH

The first person to get 20p is the winner.

Make more notes if you need them.

Collect
£15

Collect
£20

Collect
£5

25

Boxes

Find someone to play boxes with you.

We take turns to draw a line.

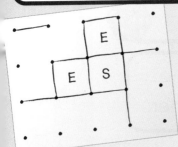

If my line makes a box, I put my letter in it...

and draw another line.

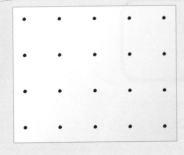

_____ got _____ boxes

_____ got _____ boxes

Total: _____ boxes

_____ got _____ boxes

_____ got _____ boxes

Total: _____ boxes

_____ got _____ boxes

_____ got _____ boxes

Total: ____ boxes

_____ got _____ boxes

_____ got _____ boxes

Total: ____ boxes

_____ got _____ boxes

_____ got _____ boxes

Total: ____ boxes

_____ got _____ boxes

_____ got _____ boxes

Total: ____ boxes

You can play again if you want to. Draw your own dots in rows.

I finished these pages on _____

What comes next? Say the next three numbers.

14, 12, 10, 8, …

6, 4, 2

What comes next?
Write the next three numbers.

41, 40, 39, 38, _____, _____, _____.

54, 53, 52, 51, _____, _____, _____.

27, 26, 25, 24, _____, _____, _____.

28, 26, 24, 22, _____, _____, _____.

42, 40, 38, 36, _____, _____, _____.

36, 34, 32, 30, _____, _____, _____.

I finished this page on _____

Play "Hopping Frogs".

Or Tiddlywinks with counters.

Score 3 points
for each frog or counter you get in the dish.

Maya got
2 frogs in.

3 + 3 = ____

Sunesh scored
9 points!

How many
counters? ____

I played this game on

----------------------------------   ----------------------------------

I like using ones to add up.

11p + 5p

I like using tens as well as ones. It's quicker.

11p + 5p

11p + 5p = 16p

Find two 10p coins and ten 1p coins to do some adding and taking away!

Use your coins to do these:

12p + 2p = ____ p

5p + 10p = ____ p

10p + 3p + 10p = ____ p

17p + 3p = ____ p

11p + 12p = ____ p

5p + 4p + 10p = ____ p

16p – 4p = ____ p

19p – 10p = ____ p

22p – 12p = ____ p

Check:

9p – 2p = ____ p

21p – 10p = ____ p

16p – 10p = ____ p

I finished these pages on _____

PART 3

There are eight activities in Part 3.

They will help you to practise:

- counting to 75, forwards and backwards, in 1s, 2s, 5s and 10s.
- spelling numbers to 70.
- adding and taking away with numbers up to 40...or more!
- using money.
- multiplying and dividing by 2.

Do each activity as often as you want to.

And you can still do any from Part 1 or Part 2!

Make ten

You need 16 playing cards:

Find as many ways as you can to make 10, with three cards.

☐ + ☐ + ☐ = 10   ☐ + ☐ + ☐ = 10

☐ + ☐ + ☐ = 10   ☐ + ☐ + ☐ = 10

☐ + ☐ + ☐ = 10   ☐ + ☐ + ☐ = 10

I finished this page on _____

Tens and teens

30	thirty
40	forty
50	fifty
60	sixty
70	seventy

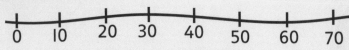

Use sums to practise your spelling.

0 10 20 30 40 50 60 70

Write the answers in words:

Ten add twenty is _____

Thirty add twenty is _____

Fifty add ten is _____

Ten add thirty is _____

Sixty add ten is _____

Be careful with 40.
It does not have a u.

4	14	40
four	fourteen	forty

Write these numbers as words:

15 _____   50 _____

17 _____   70 _____

13 _____   30 _____

14 _____   40 _____

More sums!

Thirteen add two is _____

Sixty take away ten is _____

Twenty add twenty is _____

Fourteen add two is _____

Seventy take away ten is _____

I finished these pages on _____

Ask a partner to count backwards in 5s.

I'll start at 50.
50, 45, 40, 35, 30, ...

Say "STOP" before they get to the end. Then <u>you</u> take over:

25, 20, 15, 10, 5, 0.

Do this again:
- Try counting forwards in 2s.

2, 4, 6, 8, 10, 12, 14, ...

STOP! 16, 18, 20, 22, 24, 26, 28, 30.

- Try counting backwards in 2s.

Start from 30, or 40, or 50!

Join the dots.
They go up in 2s.
Start at 0 and join 0 ⟶ 2 ⟶ 4…
<u>or</u> start at 68 and join 68 ⟶ 66 ⟶ 64…

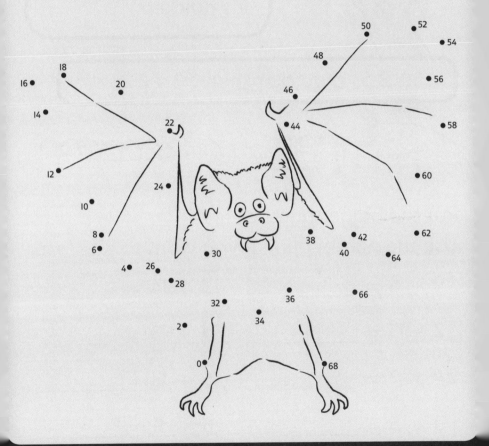

I finished this page on _____

Easier adding

When I'm adding, I often put the bigger number first, because it's quicker.

6 + 3   is quicker than   3 + 6

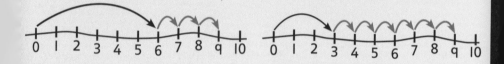

Put the bigger number first!
Use the number line if you want to.

$9 + 4 =$ _____ $3 + 14 =$ _____

$2 + 15 =$ _____ $1 + 13 =$ _____

$4 + 7 =$ _____ $5 + 13 =$ _____

$8 + 5 =$ _____ $6 + 9 =$ _____

0 1 2 3 4 5 6 7 8 9 10 11 12 13 14 15 16 17 18

Sometimes you can find <u>tens</u> when you add up three numbers.

7 + 4 + 3

7 add 3 makes 10.
10 add 4 makes 14.

Look for tens!

2 + 3 + 8 = _____   5 + 7 + 5 = _____

5 + 6 + 4 = _____   15 + 1 + 9 = _____

3 + 8 + 7 = _____   2 + 8 + 10 = _____

Ask someone to do these sums.
Ask them <u>how</u> they did them.

2 + 24 =   7 + 15 + 3 =

Did they put the bigger number first?
Did they look for tens?
Or did they use another way?

I finished this page on _____

You need 10 pieces of card
about this big:

Draw a toy for the dog on each card.

Then make a price ticket:

Dog's toys
£2 each.

Work with a partner.
Make up problems for each other.

Try these, to get you started:

I want to buy 4 toys.

How much will it cost? _____

I spent £10 on toys.

How many did I buy? _____

Dog toys

Use the cards to help you.
Check with a calculator.

4 toys at £2 each	How many for £10?
4 × 2 = ___	10 ÷ 2 = ___

I did this activity on

------------------------------   ------------------------------

Coin problems

You need three 10p coins
and fifteen 1p coins.

23p + 15p = ___ p

17p + 16p = ___ p

Use the coins and draw your own problems.
Find someone to do them!

___p + ___p = ___p

___p + ___p = ___p

2

Use coins to do this:

I had 40p. I spent 27p.

He had ____p left.

Make up your own problems.
Find someone to do them!

I had ____p.

I spent ____p.

She had ____p left.

I had ____p.

I spent ____p.

She had ____p left.

I had ____p.

I spent ____p.

He had ____p left.

I had ____p.

I spent ____p.

He had ____p left.

I finished this page on _____

Find my number

I'm thinking of a number.
You have to work out what it is.

Ask me: Is it bigger than _____?
<u>or</u> Is it smaller than _____?

Is it bigger than 20?

No

Is it bigger than 10?

No

Is it bigger than 5?

Yes

So it must be 6, 7, 8, 9 or 10...

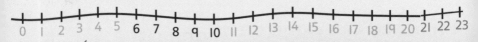

0 1 2 3 4 5 6 7 8 9 10 11 12 13 14 15 16 17 18 19 20 21 22 23

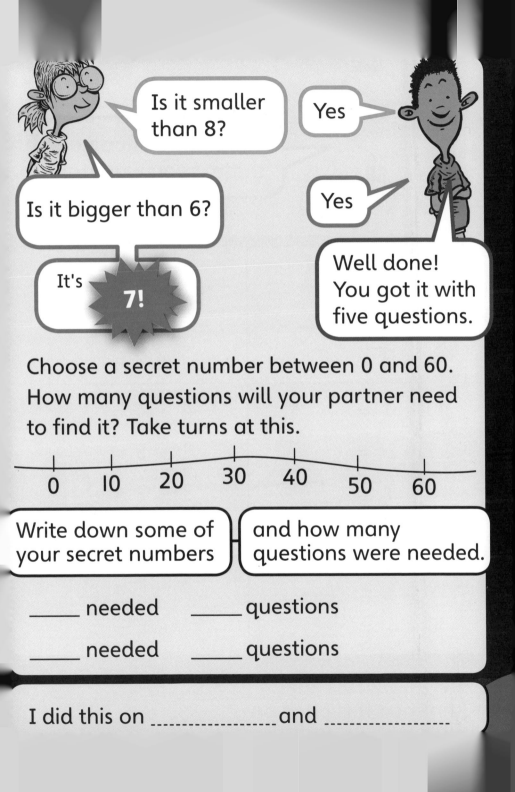

Is it smaller than 8?

Yes

Is it bigger than 6?

Yes

It's 7!

Well done! You got it with five questions.

Choose a secret number between 0 and 60. How many questions will your partner need to find it? Take turns at this.

0   10   20   30   40   50   60

Write down some of your secret numbers and how many questions were needed.

_____ needed   _____ questions

_____ needed   _____ questions

I did this on _____ and _____

Quick sums

Time yourself doing these if you want to!

2 + 4 = ____	8 + 1 = ____
5 + 0 = ____	7 + 3 = ____
4 + 5 = ____	3 + 2 = ____
10 – 0 = ____	4 – 4 = ____
7 – 2 = ____	9 – 5 = ____
8 – 3 = ____	3 – 2 = ____
2 + 8 = ____	3 + 5 = ____
6 – 3 = ____	2 – 1 = ____
6 + 4 = ____	1 + 1 = ____

I finished this page on ------------------------------------

46

Last page

Leave this page until you have done __all__ the other pages!

Tick the things you can do.

- I can count 70 things.

- I can count backwards from 70 to 0.

  70, 69, 68, ...

- I can count in 2s to 50.

- I can count in 5s to 50.

- I can spell numbers one to seventy.

- I can add and take away with numbers up to 40.

Well done!

I finished this page on _____

Rapid Maths is a mathematics course designed specifically for 6 to 11 year olds. Each part of the Home Maths book can be used for a whole term to support classroom work. The activities can be done in any order, and many can be done more than once.

Designed and produced by Debbie Oatley @ room9design
Original illustrations © Pearson Education Ltd 2009
Illustrated by Martin Chatterton, Pet Gotohda and Matt Buckley
Cover illustration © Pearson Education Ltd
Cover illustration by Martin Chatterton
Printed in Malaysia (CTP-PJB)

Acknowledgements
We would like to thank Sheriff Hutton Primary School, Sheriff Hutton; Queens Dyke Primary School, Witney and Kirtlington CE School, Kirtlington for their invaluable help in the development and trialling of this book.

The author and publisher would like to thank the following individuals and organisations for permission to reproduce photographs:
©Shutterstock / Losevsky Powell: p.2 (buttons);
©Shutterstock / Ana de Sousa: p.2 (buttons);
©Shutterstock / Francseco Abrignani: p.16;
©Shutterstock / Francseco Abrignani: p.17;
©Shutterstock / Francseco Abrignani: p.33.
All other photos © Pearson Education Ltd / Clark Wiseman, Studio 8.

Every effort has been made to contact copyright holders of material reproduced in this book. Any omissions will be rectified in subsequent printings if notice is given to the publishers.

Heinemann is an imprint of Pearson Education Limited, a company incorporated in England and Wales, having its registered office at Edinburgh Gate, Harlow, Essex, CM20 2JE. Registered company number: 872828

www.heinemann.co.uk

Heinemann is a registered trademark of Pearson Education Limited

Text © Rose Griffiths 2009

First published 2009

14
10 9 8

British Library Cataloguing in Publication Data
A catalogue record for this book is available from the British Library.

ISBN 978 0 435 91236 9

Heinemann is part of

PEARSON

T 0845 630 22 22
F 0845 630 77 77
myorders@pearson.com
www.pearsonschools.co.uk

ISBN 978-0-435-91236-9

9 780435 912369

Heinemann